PLANET IN CRISIS
CLIMATE CRISIS

This edition published in 2009 by:
The Rosen Publishing Group, Inc.
29 East 21st Street
New York, NY 10010

Designed and produced by
David West Books

Editor: James Pickering
Picture Research: Carlotta Cooper

Photo Credits: Abbreviations: t-top, m-middle, b-bottom, r-right,
l-left, c-center.

Front cover, tl (Sipa Press); 4t, 20t, 25t NASA; 3, 14–15 & 24b - Corbis Images. Pages 4–5, 8t, m & b, 9tl &
m, 15ml, bl, mr & br, 17m, 24t, 28r, 30 - Corbis Images; 5t, 24–25 (Sabine Vielmo); 5bl (Andy Crump); 6–7,
12r, 18–19, 23t- Rex Features Ltd.; 6br, 29t (Mark Edwards); 7t (Roland Seitre); 9b (Shehzad Noorani); 10m
(D. Escartin); 10b (Voltchev/UNEP); 11t (Klaus Andrews); 12l (Horst Schafer); 15t (Romain Garrouste); 16b
(Ron Giling); 17t (mrlins); 18 (Porcelain Monkey Garage); 19l U.S. Department of State; 20b (Julio Etchart);
20–21 (Peres/UNEP); 23r (Mathieu Laboureur); 28b (Jorgen Schytte); 5br & 17mr (Peter MacDiarmid); 6b,
11b, 19r, 21m & b (Sipa Press); 7bl & b (2002 Eumetsat); 9tr (Richard Jones); 13 (Monika Duscher); 16bl
(Greg Williams); 22l (Solent News and Photos); 24t (Ray Tang); 25bl (Action Press); 25br World Resources
Institute; 26 NOAA; 26–27t (Markus Schweiss); 26–27b U.S. Department of Energy; 27 Dartmouth Electron
Microscope Facility-Dartmouth College; 29r (Eric Draper); 29bl (fogcat5); 29bm (David G. Romero).

Library of Congress Cataloging-in-Publication Data

Parker, Russ, 1970-
 Climate crisis / Russ Parker.
     p. cm. -- (Planet in crisis)
 Includes bibliographical references and index.
 ISBN 978-1-4358-5254-9 (lib. bdg.) -- ISBN 978-1-4358-0684-9 (pbk.) -- ISBN 978-1-4358-0690-0 (6-pack)
 1. Climatic changes--Juvenile literature. 2. Global warming--Juvenile literature. 3. Greenhouse effect,
Atmospheric--Juvenile literature. I. Title.
 QC981.8.C5P37 2009
 551.6--dc22

                          2008043614

Printed and bound in China

First published in Great Britain by Heinemann Library, a division of Reed Educational and Professional Publishing Limited.

PLANET IN CRISIS

CLIMATE CRISIS

Russ Parker

rosen publishing's
rosen central

New York

CONTENTS

The "ozone hole" (purple) shows thinning of the protective ozone layer high over the South Pole in 2006. The hole allows more of the Sun's harmful rays to enter.

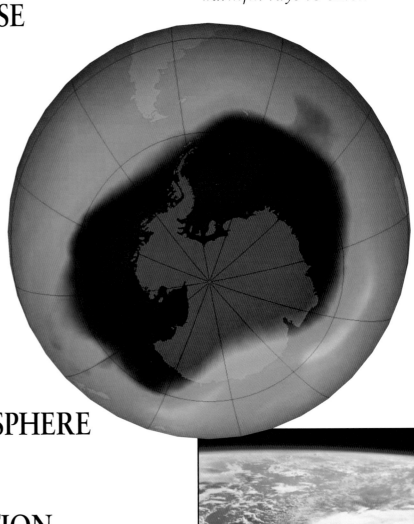

Great storms such as hurricanes are becoming more powerful, common, and widespread.

INTRODUCTION

"Here is the weather forecast: Tomorrow there will be sleet, blizzards, snowdrifts, and a wind-chill of minus 20 degrees Fahrenheit, followed by a hurricane, heatwave, and severe drought. The day after should be fine." Our day-to-day weather changes faster than ever. The climate—the general long-term patterns of weather around the world over months and years—does too. Human activity is the main cause, especially the pollution, chemicals, and gases we release into the air. Can our planet cope with this crisis?

Carbon dioxide (CO_2) is one of the main greenhouse gases that cause global warming. Whenever we burn anything, we make more CO_2.

Demonstrators warn that, as global warming melts polar ice, sea levels may rise enough to flood whole islands.

6 THE WEATHER FORECAST

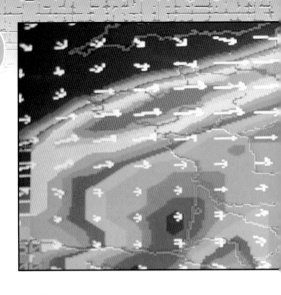

Sometimes the weather changes hourly, from blizzard conditions to bright sunshine. At other times it stays settled for weeks. Scientists called meteorologists measure weather worldwide in order to make forecasts and discover more about climate change.

USEFUL PREDICTIONS

Predicting the weather is vital for many reasons. Pilots, sailors, farmers, skiers, climbers, and many others arrange their work and leisure around the weather. Ignoring it could be fatal.

Being GREEN

Instruments provide information for weather forecasting in places that have extreme climates. The barometer measures air pressure, while the hygrometer determines humidity levels. The anemometer calculates wind speed and direction.

Harsh weather, like snowstorms in New York City, bring normal life to a halt. Disruption costs billions of dollars—and sometimes lives too.

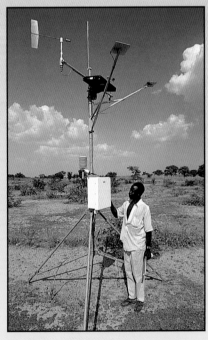

Weather station in Africa

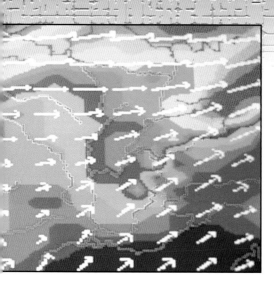

Some of the world's biggest super-computers analyze and display weather information (left).

Instruments on radiosondes ("weather balloons") radio information back to ground stations.

Since 2002, Meteosat satellites (inset) have been put into orbit by Ariane rockets. Their cameras detect light rays, infrared (heat), ultraviolet, and the radio and microwaves used for radar. The results are analyzed in control rooms to identify weather patterns.

SHORT AND LONG TERM

Meteorologists use a vast array of technologies, from simple thermometers for temperature, to billion-dollar satellites that detect rain, fog, wind patterns, and the height of ocean waves to the nearest few centimeters. Day-to-day weather measurements build up to help predict longer-term changes in climate over many years.

8 GLOBAL CLIMATES

Climates around the world are affected by many features, from the shape of Earth and the way it goes around the Sun, to winds and ocean currents.

SHAPE AND ORBIT

Earth is ball-shaped. The middle regions, called the tropics, are nearer the Sun and receive more warmth. The Earth also goes around the Sun, not in a circle, but in an oval-like ellipse. When closest to the Sun, we have warm summers.

MOVING CURRENTS

As the Earth spins around once each day, the Sun heats different parts of it in different amounts. Warm air rises, cooler air flows along to take its place, and this sets up patterns of winds. Ocean currents form in the same way.

Cold climates
Areas near the poles have short, warm summers and long, cold winters.

Dry climates
Most deserts form on either side of the tropics. They receive winds which have lost all their moisture.

Over thousands of years, plants and animals have adapted to the climate in their part of the world. For example, as winds blow moist warm air over mountains, the air rises and cools. The moisture falls as rain, so lush plants can grow. As the wind blows onwards, it gets drier. The land here receives little rain, so deserts form.

Polar climates
The bottom and top of the world are icy-cold all year.

Temperate climates
Midway between the poles and the Equator are warm summers and cool winters, with few extremes.

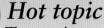

Hot topic
To survive comfortably in changing climates, living things adapt —including people. Light-colored, loose robes soak up less heat and allow air to move freely around the body, keeping it cooler.

Cool robes for the hot Sun

Mountain climates
Temperatures fall with height. Mountains are cool in summer and freezing in winter.

Equator

WHY THE TROPICS ARE HOT

At midday, the Sun shines almost directly overhead in the tropics. Its rays pass through less atmosphere than the slanting rays of polar regions, which means less heat loss. More of the Sun's heat gets through to the surface and is concentrated into a small area, so tropical climates are hotter.

Moist tropical climates
It's warm throughout the year and very wet in the monsoon season.

Polar — Sun's rays spread out

Temperate

Equator — Sun's rays concentrated in smaller area

Temperate

Polar — Sun's rays spread out

9

CLIMATES LONG AGO

Seasons change, mainly with warm summers and cold winters. But 200 million years ago, at the time of the dinosaurs, the Earth's climate was very different. There were hardly any seasons.

MANY CHANGES

Since the Earth's beginning, 4.5 billion years ago, climates have been constantly changing. Sometimes the whole world was warm and wet, and lush plants thrived in steamy swamps—even at the poles. At other times the Earth was cold all over.

Today the Sahara Desert is spreading across North Africa (main picture). Yet the cave paintings of ancient people (inset) depict the Sahara region just a few thousand years ago, with wild cattle and lions in woods, and even hippos and crocodiles in the rivers and swamps.

Some polar ice is more than 14,000 feet deep, made of snow from half a million years ago. Drills bring up rod-like ice cores with tiny trapped air bubbles showing the atmosphere's make-up long ago.

Sampling ice in the Arctic

MANY ICE AGES

There have been dozens of ice ages during prehistory. The last one began over 140,000 years ago. As the Earth cooled, ice sheets spread from the poles across much of North America, Europe, and northern Asia. Wildlife had to adapt or move south. This Great Ice Age had almost faded away 10,000 years ago.

Greatest spread of ice sheets

In the Great Ice Age, 18,000 years ago, half of the Earth froze. Mammoths evolved woolly coats to cope (right).

CLUES TO THE PAST

Information about past climates comes from the types of rocks formed at the time. It also comes from fossils—the remains of long-dead plants and animals, preserved in rocks and turned to stone. Most climate changes were very gradual. Plants and animals were able to adapt slowly or spread to more suitable areas.

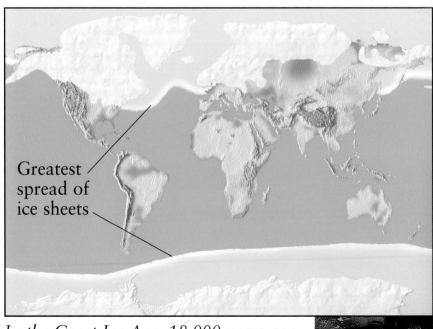

Some people talk about the "greenhouse effect" of global warming as if it is a brand new feature of our world. In one sense, it isn't. What is the greenhouse effect, and why is it changing?

KEEPING THE EARTH WARM

Glass lets light in and out, but not heat. A garden greenhouse lets in the Sun's light rays. Inside, some of this light energy is reflected or soaked up by objects and naturally converted to heat or infrared rays. This warmth is then trapped inside the glass and builds up, making the greenhouse hotter from within.

Hot topic
Earth with its natural greenhouse effect is more than 50°F warmer than without it. But that's a tiny amount compared to the planet Venus. Most of the atmosphere there is carbon dioxide, which is a very effective greenhouse gas. It traps so much heat that on Venus, the average temperature is a scorching 870°F—hot enough for wood to catch fire. Studying Venus can help scientists predict what may happen here on Earth.

"Hothouse" Venus

The average temperature over the whole Earth through an entire year is 60°F. Without the natural greenhouse effect to trap the Sun's energy, it would be just 5°F!

THE NATURAL GREENHOUSE EFFECT

The Earth's atmosphere is a mixture of gases: mainly nitrogen (78%) and oxygen (21%), plus tiny amounts of argon, carbon dioxide, and others. Some of the Sun's energy which is not heat is absorbed and converted into heat, both in the atmosphere and at the surface. This raises the overall temperature, but only to a certain level. Beyond this, more heat would be lost to space than is received from the Sun, so the Earth would cool. In this natural greenhouse effect, incoming energy balances outgoing energy.

On a sunny day inside a real greenhouse, it may be 30°F warmer than outside. This is not due to the Sun's heat coming in, but to its light, which is changed to heat.

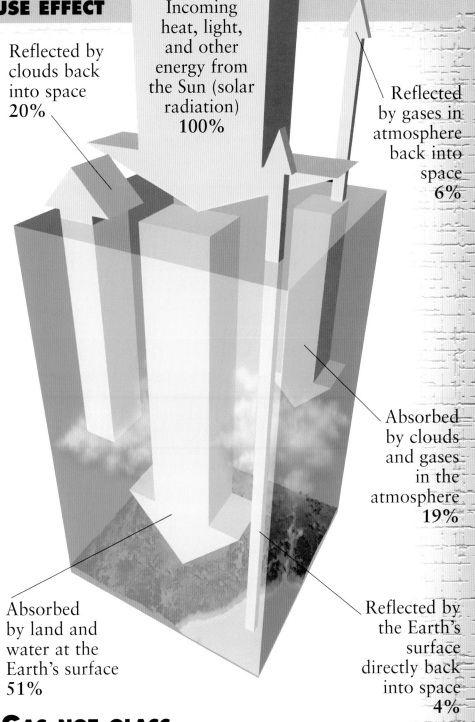

Reflected by clouds back into space
20%

Incoming heat, light, and other energy from the Sun (solar radiation)
100%

Reflected by gases in atmosphere back into space
6%

Absorbed by clouds and gases in the atmosphere
19%

Absorbed by land and water at the Earth's surface
51%

Reflected by the Earth's surface directly back into space
4%

GAS NOT GLASS

Earth is like a greenhouse, but with gas rather than glass. Some of the Sun's non-heat energy is changed into heat and trapped by greenhouse gases in the atmosphere. This has occurred in a steady, balanced way for a very long time.

PROBLEM GASES

The Earth's natural greenhouse effect is becoming unnatural. We pump huge amounts of heat-trapping gases into the air, which wrap the Earth in a thick "blanket." Disastrous results include global warming (see following pages).

CARBON DIOXIDE

Carbon dioxide (CO_2) makes up only 0.03% (1/3,000th) of the atmosphere. But it is an effective greenhouse gas since it traps a lot of heat. Every form of burning produces it, and this is the main reason its levels are rising rapidly.

MAIN GREENHOUSE GASES

Carbon dioxide is important because we produce so much of it daily. Chlorofluorocarbons (CFCs) are used in refrigeration, air conditioning, industrial cleaners, and foam-type packaging. They trap 20,000 times more heat than CO_2, but their quantities are much smaller.

Carbon dioxide 49%

Nitrous oxide 6%

Ozone 12%

Methane 18%

CFCs 15%

General industry 30%

In an industrialized nation such as the U.S., over one-third of the CO_2 released into the atmosphere is from burning fuels like gas, coal, and oil to generate electricity. Almost as much comes from gasoline, diesel, jet, and other engines, in various forms of transportation. Factory furnaces and ovens account for about one-quarter. Central heating, stoves, and fireplaces in the home represent about one-tenth of CO_2 emissions.

Transportation 28%

Hot topic

Clearing forests is a double disaster for the climate. Burning the unwanted wood creates one-fifth of global CO_2 emissions. Living trees take in CO_2 and use it for growth—but not when they are gone.

Forest trees help to lower CO_2 in the atmosphere.

OTHER GREENHOUSE GASES

Other heat-trapping gases include nitrous oxide, especially from coal-fired power stations, and ozone, produced in smog over traffic-choked cities. Another is methane. It comes from burnt wood. It is also made naturally by vegetative decay in bogs and swamps and by digestion in plant-eating animals.

Power stations 30%

Homes 12%

Cows, sheep, and other plant-eaters release methane during digestion. More farm animals = more methane.

1

6 WARMER WORLD

Since we began measuring temperatures accurately, the warmest years have been mainly in the past two decades. It is likely that records will continue to be broken.

GLOBAL WARMING

Increasing amounts of greenhouse gases in the atmosphere (see previous page) are making our world hotter. This is called global warming. Some people still insist that it has not begun and may never start. But it's here, now. Average world temperatures have risen by almost one degree Fahrenheit in the past century.

(see previous page)

Hot topic

Many small island nations, especially in the Pacific, have land that is just a few feet above sea level. As global warming takes hold and sea levels rise, some of these may slowly disappear under the waves. One of the first may be Tuvalu (formerly the Ellice Islands) near Samoa.

WORLD TEMPERATURE

This chart shows the world's average surface temperature each year for the past 150 years. There are small rises and falls here and there, but the general trend is an accelerating increase.

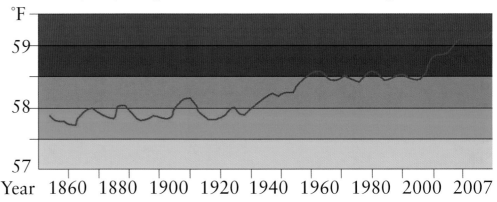

°F

59

58

57

Year 1860 1880 1900 1920 1940 1960 1980 2000 2007

More droughts have affected more regions in the past 30 years than in the 50 years before. Africa has been hit especially hard. When rains fail to fall, famines can strike already starving populations, killing millions. Unlike Africa, developed countries often have emergency food and water reserves in times of drought.

Tuvalu – first drowned nation?

SPEEDING UP

Scientists predict that if we continue making yet more greenhouse gases, global warming will happen faster, by 5 to 7°F in the next fifty years. Even if we stop these gases now, the rise could be 1°F over 25 years. This may not sound like much, but it could have devastating effects, such as shifting rainfall patterns. What is now rich, well-watered farmland might become parched desert, unable to grow our food.

WHEN ICE MELTS

Gigantic amounts of water are frozen into ice sheets at the poles, especially at Antarctica. As global warming continues and ice melts into the ocean, sea levels will rise. Vast areas of land around the world's coasts, including great cities and ports and the homes of millions, are just a few feet above average sea level. A predicted sea level rise of 15–20 inches in the next 50 years will flood so much coastal land that half a billion people could be made homeless and jobless.

A protester (above, right) warns of rising seas, and long-term predictions suggest great cities like Miami will drown.

After a 15-feet rise in sea level.

1

EXTREME WEATHER

Almost every week there is news of a natural disaster due to violent or unusual weather. Are these events becoming more common?

MORE EXTREME

There have always been gales, tornadoes, hurricanes, downpours, and similar powerful weather. But they have increased greatly in recent years. Places where disasters often occur are used to coping with typical damage associated with them. But now the events are more destructive and happen in more places which are unprepared.

In 2005, Hurricane Rita hit the Gulf Coast causing huge damage in Louisiana and Texas, including seven deaths.

Many tropical places have regular storms with thunder, lightning, and heavy rain. But changes are happening fast as rainfall becomes heavier and winds blow more strongly.

EL NIÑO – "THE CHILD"

People fishing along South America's west coast noticed that every few years, their catches were reduced. This is due to changes in a huge ocean current called *El Niño*, "The Child," because it begins during the Christmas season. Winds and currents combine to bring warmer, nutrient-poor water across the Pacific and along the Equator to replace the more typical nutrient-rich, cooler current that sustains fish.

NORMAL YEAR

Air circulation of trade winds

Warmer water

EL NIÑO YEAR

Air circulation splits in two

Current

Warmer water spreads east

CHANGES IN NATURE

Global warming is affecting nature too. Flowers bloom earlier in spring, birds migrate later in fall, and insects that used to sleep through the cold season still buzz about in winter. This will also affect people greatly. Mosquitoes, ticks, and other warmth-loving pests that carry diseases are spreading into new areas.

Cyclone Nargis flooded immense regions of Burma (Myanmar) in May 2008. More than 150,000 people are known to have lost their lives.

WORLDWIDE EFFECTS OF *EL NIÑO*

El Niño is part of a huge weather system that has effects across the tropics. Droughts affect India (1), Sri Lanka and Indonesia (2), killing crops, and Australia (3), causing bush fires. Cyclone storms hit Pacific islands such as Tahiti (4). Unusually warm water harms coral reefs (5). Downpours and floods affect North America's west coast (6) and the Gulf of Mexico (7), and also South America (8), where the fishing industry is ruined (9). Droughts and floods even hit parts of Africa (10).

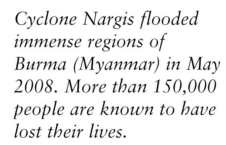

Wetter

Drier

Hotter

Equator

AIR POLLUTION

On a clear day, views can be spectacular. But we have fewer clear days now, due to smoke and fumes from power stations, factory smokestacks, vehicles, and forest fires.

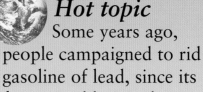

Hot topic
Some years ago, people campaigned to rid gasoline of lead, since its fumes could cause brain damage. Now attention has shifted to other chemicals and tiny bits called particulates, which damage the lungs.

POLLUTION WE CAN SEE

Some of the gases that pollute the atmosphere, such as CFCs (shown on the next page), are invisible. Others, especially exhaust fumes from vehicle engines, carry tiny particulates. These cause a dusty haze, made worse when chemicals in the fumes react to form smog that covers cities.

Cities such as Los Angeles and Mexico City are surrounded by hills. Calm weather traps vehicle fumes in the mountain basins. The fumes change in sunlight into damaging low-level ozone and choking smog.

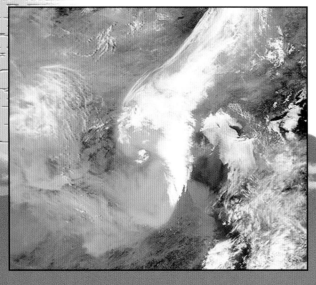

The "Asian Brown Cloud" has spread across the Pacific Ocean and south to Australia.

HEALTH PROBLEMS

In recent years, a vast new problem has affected much of India and Southeast Asia. Called the "Asian Brown Cloud" (see opposite), it is due to weak winds mixing fumes from traffic, power stations, factories, and burning logged forests to clear them for farmland. As a result, people suffer from asthma, breathing problems, and lung infections like bronchitis.

Traffic pollution can kill.

In 1991, the Philippines' Mount Pinatubo volcano erupted, showering the area with thick ash. The ash also blasted high into the atmosphere, spreading around the world and causing two years of cooler, cloudier weather.

Ozone (O_3) is a form of the gas oxygen, O_2. High in the atmosphere, it screens out some of the the Sun's harmful rays. Low down near the ground, in traffic smog, it causes health problems and adds to the greenhouse effect.

LESS OZONE

The ozone layer is a region of ozone-rich gases high above the Earth's surface. It protects us from the Sun's harmful ultraviolet (UV) rays. It has been damaged by polluting gases, especially CFCs, as shown opposite. Worldwide control of CFC emissions will hopefully allow the natural ozone layer to repair itself over the next 50-100 years.

Hot topic
As the atmospheric ozone thins, it allows through more ultraviolet radiation from the Sun. This harms not only people, but plants and animals too. At present, the main ozone loss is above the poles, where few people live, and the thinning varies from year to year. If the loss spreads, it could affect millions of people in both northern and southern lands.

UV causes sunburn.

CFCs were used in older refrigeration equipment.

The gases called CFCs "eat" ozone. Each CFC (1) breaks down in the atmosphere to release its chlorine atom (2). This joins to a molecule of ozone, O_3 (3) and "snaps off" one of the oxygen atoms to leave normal oxygen, O_2 (4). Then the chlorine releases its oxygen atom, O (5). The single atoms collect and join in pairs to form more normal oxygen (6), while the chlorine is ready to carry out the whole process again (7). The worst-affected area is over the South Pole (left). It is not an empty ozone "hole" but a depletion or thinning of ozone in its layer.

Thinned ozone over Antarctica (purple)

Continual loss and production of ozone normally keeps its level steady. Energy in the Sun's rays (A) splits particles or molecules of ozone (B) into normal oxygen molecules (C) and single atoms (D). But these join together to form ozone again (E).

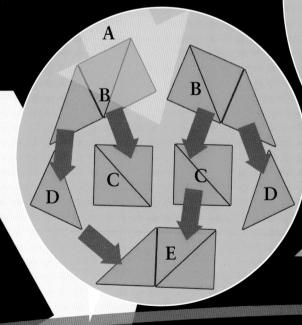

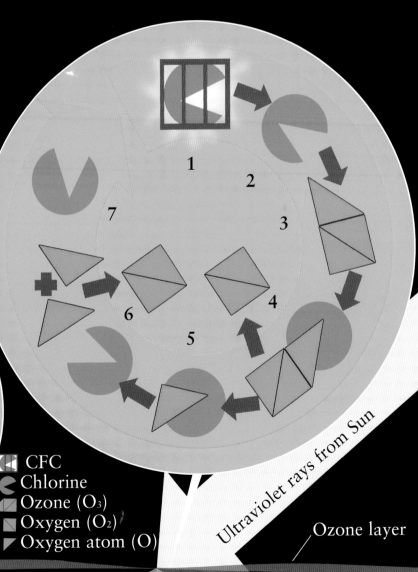

CFC
Chlorine
Ozone (O_3)
Oxygen (O_2)
Oxygen atom (O)

Ultraviolet rays from Sun

Ozone layer

CFCs from
Earth

The climate crisis is a worldwide problem. Storms and floods do not stop at a nation's borders. Although all nations suffer, some countries cause more harm than others.

THE ROLE OF CARBON

One way of assessing the problem is by carbon emissions—amounts of carbon dioxide and other greenhouse gases produced by burning. Some places are introducing "carbon taxes." If you burn more, you pay more.

Costumed demonstrators protest the U.S.'s major contribution to global warming and its government's reluctance to cut emissions.

CARBON CULPRITS

Until recently, the U.S. was the biggest emitter of CO_2. Its high standard of living relies on burning oil-based fuels in power stations, cars, factories, and for heating. In 2007, China took the top spot. India and other fast-growing nations in East Asia are also catching up fast.

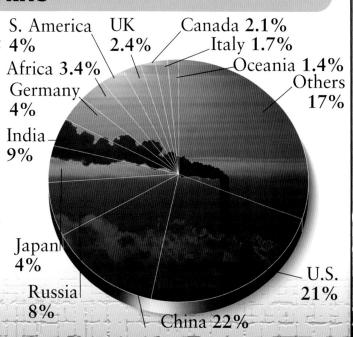

S. America 4%
UK 2.4%
Canada 2.1%
Italy 1.7%
Africa 3.4%
Germany 4%
Oceania 1.4%
Others 17%
India 9%
Japan 4%
Russia 8%
U.S. 21%
China 22%

Being GREEN

Satellites "spy" on the whole globe. They can detect a forest being cleared by burning, which destroys wildlife and produces damaging smoke and greenhouse gases. The culprits can be pinpointed and encouraged to become more "green" in the future.

Satellites: "spies in space"

Conservationists use many tactics to publicize problems like global warming. This power station cooling tower in Germany has become a "screen" for a huge light show.

The 1998 Kyoto agreement tried to limit greenhouse gas emissions. Most countries signed up. The U.S. is the only developed nation not to join.

RICH AND POOR

Instead of sharing them with other nations, developed countries use up valuable energy sources, like coal and petroleum, at a rate that cannot go on forever. As they do so, they pollute the atmosphere for all. International meetings are held to draft laws where countries emitting the most carbon try to reduce it most. But agreements are often weak and do little to solve the crisis.

Former U.S. vice president Al Gore (1993–2001) has gained worldwide fame as an environmental campaigner against global warming, especially with his documentary An Inconvenient Truth *(2006).*

CARBON CAPTURE

The chief greenhouse gas is carbon dioxide, given off mainly by burning fuels such as oil, gas, coal, and wood. If we can somehow trap this carbon dioxide, would that help to slow its increase in the atmosphere and lessen the effects of climate change?

HIDING CARBON UNDERGROUND

Several technologies aim to capture and store, or sequester, carbon dioxide from burning fuel. In one method, the carbon dioxide is forced down a hole drilled far underground, where it passes into spongy rock for long-term storage. Air and steam can be pressure-injected down a hole to a coal seam, to force coal gas, a useful fuel, back up another hole.

Hot topic
Carbon dioxide from combustion or burning could be stored for a time by dissolving it in the vast waters of the oceans. But this would make the waters acidic, which could harm sea plants, animals, and other marine life.

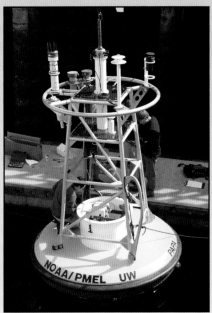

Checking the sea's acidity

Power station

Waste gas pipeline

CO_2 gas

Coal gas

Injected air and steam

Coal seam

Underground fire

CO_2 store

The U.S.'s planned FutureGen zero-emission power station (below) had government funding cut in 2008. It may go ahead with private funds.

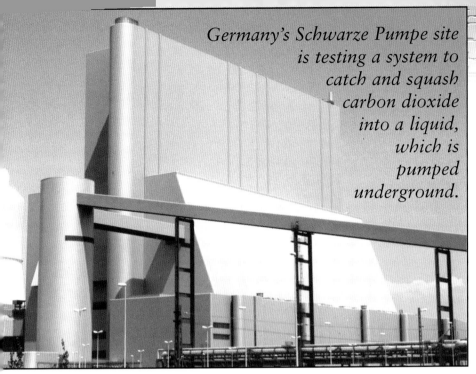

Germany's Schwarze Pumpe site is testing a system to catch and squash carbon dioxide into a liquid, which is pumped underground.

TRADE IN CARBON

Various schemes around the world encourage companies and industries to reduce carbon emissions by allowing them "carbon credits." If they go above a certain level of emission, they have to pay penalties. Companies with spare credits can make money by selling them to others.

REDUCING EMISSIONS

Reducing our burning of fuels for power stations, heating, and transportation would lessen carbon emissions. Another method is to burn biofuels made from plant materials. The advantage to using plants as fuel is that when plants are growing they remove and absorb carbon dioxide from the atmosphere.

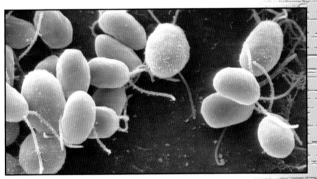

Like all plants, microscopic algae take in carbon dioxide to live and grow. Studying their genes may help us to discover new ways to capture carbon.

CLEAN UP THE ATMOSPHERE

The world is so huge, and its weather is so vast and complicated—can individual people help to clean up the air and restore the climate's natural balance?

No time to lose

Yes! Many people are not aware of how the crisis will affect their world and their future. Start by spreading information about climate change. Even if we stop releasing all greenhouse and ozone-damaging gases today, world weather will still get hotter and more violent for many years. There's no time to lose.

Hot topic

All types of burning, even renewable "green" biofuels like bio-diesel, make greenhouse gases. Nuclear power is almost zero-emission in this respect. But it has many other problems and possible hazards.

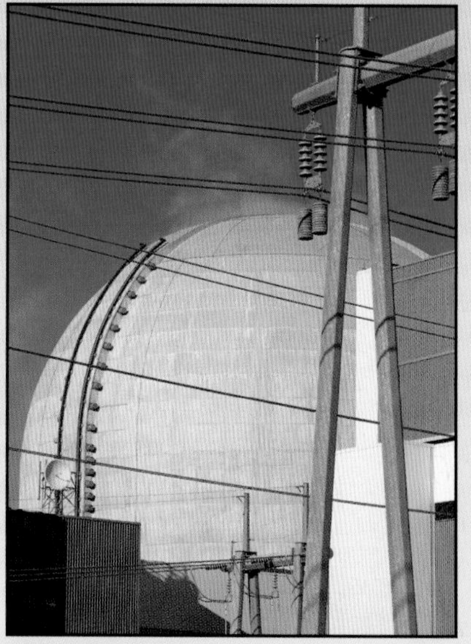

Nuclear is "non-carbon."

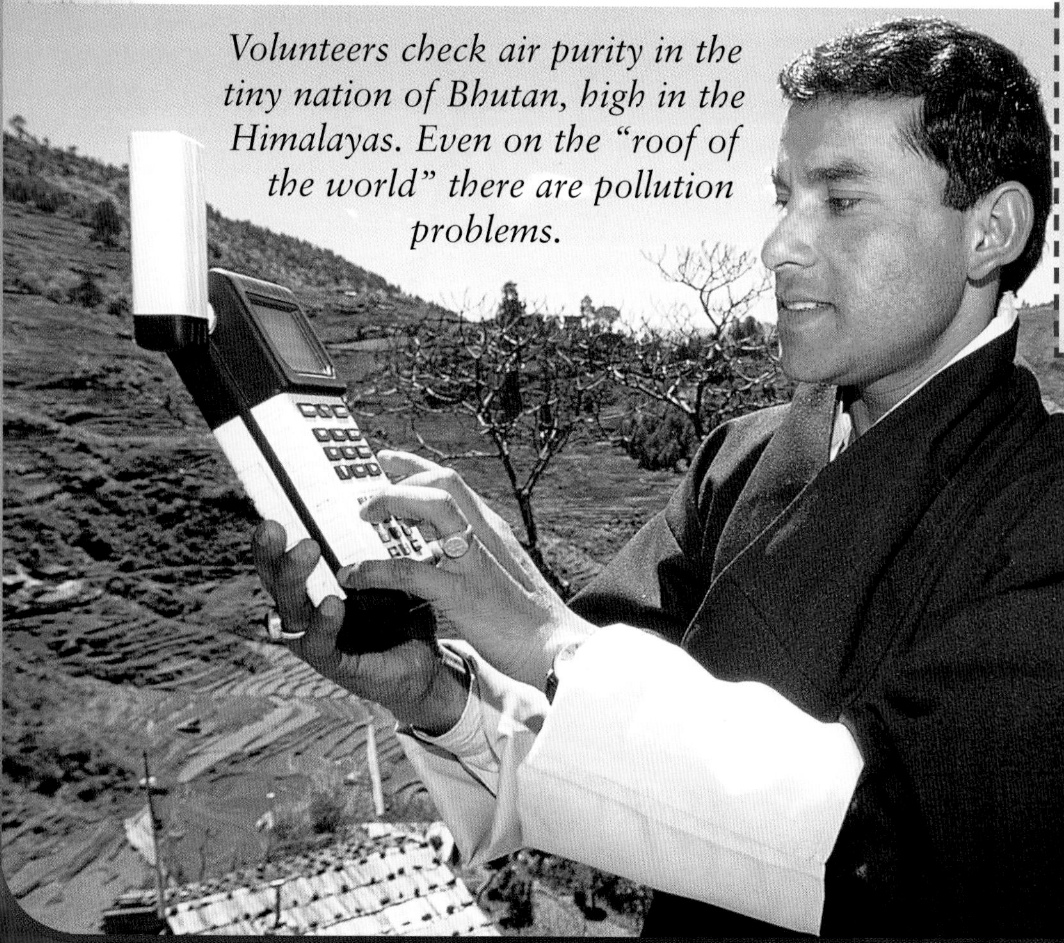

Volunteers check air purity in the tiny nation of Bhutan, high in the Himalayas. Even on the "roof of the world" there are pollution problems.

Forests destroyed by logging and clearing are being replanted for the future in the Rishi Valley, in India's Chittoor District.

THE CARBON BALANCE

If more carbon-based gases like carbon dioxide in the atmosphere cause global warming, would less carbon do the reverse? In order to live and grow, trees and other plants absorb carbon dioxide from air and energy from sunlight. Forests are "carbon sinks," moving carbon from the atmosphere to within themselves. It's another good reason to save the trees we have and plant many more.

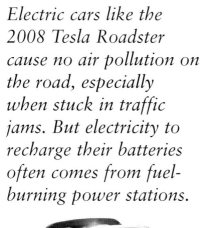

Electric cars like the 2008 Tesla Roadster cause no air pollution on the road, especially when stuck in traffic jams. But electricity to recharge their batteries often comes from fuel-burning power stations.

In the 2000s, the Governor of California, Arnold Schwarzenegger, began to sign new laws designed both to reduce carbon emissions and persuade others of the dangers of global warming.

The climate crisis is very complex. Excess greenhouse gases leading to global warming, rising sea levels, more violent storms, smog and air pollution, ozone problems, shifting weather patterns, droughts here, floods there ...

A DIFFICULT FORECAST

It is very difficult to be sure how climate change will affect us in the future. Governments need to take action now and maybe our future tomorrows will be brighter and clearer. You can raise awareness of the problems by discussing them in school.

FOR MORE INFORMATION

Organizations

Educational Gobal Climate Modeling (EDGCM)
http://edgcm.columbia.edu/
The EdGCM project develops global climate models that can be downloaded and run on desktop computers.

EPA GLOBAL WARMING KIDS' SITE
http://www.epa.gov/globalwarming/kids/
The U.S. Environmental Protection Agency's (EPA) website for younger people, full of information.

FRIENDS OF THE EARTH
1717 Massachusetts Avenue
Suite 600
Washington, DC 20036
(202) 783-7400
www.foe.org/
The largest international network of environmental groups, campaigning for the conservation of species and wild places.

NASA - JET PROPULSION LABORATORY
California Institute of Technology
4800 Oak Grove Drive
Pasadena, CA 91109
(818) 354-4321
http://climate.jpl.nasa.gov/
A NASA website that uses interactive graphics to explain some of the issues relating to our changing climate.

NATIONAL OCEANIC AND ATMOSPHERIC ADMINISTRATION (NOAA)
National Climatic Data Center
151 Patton Avenue
Asheville, NC 28801-5001
(828) 271-4800
www.ncdc.noaa.gov/oa/climate/globalwarming.html
A NOAA website that uses its own data and that of the Intergovernmental Panel on Climate Change to answer frequently asked questions about climate change.

For further reading

David, Laurie and Cambria Gordon. *The Down to Earth Guide to Global Warming*. New York, NY: Scholastic, 2007.

Cheel, Richard. *Global Warming Alert!* (Disaster Alert!). New York, NY: Crabtree Publishing Company, 2007.

Gore, Al. *An Inconvenient Truth: The Crisis of Global Warming*. New York, NY: Viking Children's Books/ Rodale Books, 2007.

Simpson, Kathleen. National Geographic *Investigates: Extreme Weather: Science Tackles Global Warming and Climate Change*. Washington, DC: National Geographic Society, 2008.

Kowalski, Kathiann M. *Global Warming* (Open for Debate). New York, NY: Benchmark Books, 2004.

Miller, Debra A. *Global Warming* (Hot Topics). Farmington Hills, MI: Lucent Books, 2008.

Web Sites

Due to the changing nature of Internet links, Rosen Publishing has developed an online list of Web sites related to the subject of this book. This site is updated regularly. Please use this link to access the list: http://www.rosenlinks.com/pic/clim

GLOSSARY

atmosphere
The layer of air that surrounds the planet Earth. It becomes thinner with height, and above 300 miles fades away into the vast unknown of space.

CFCs
Chlorofluorocarbons or industrial chemicals which have an especially damaging effect on ozone in the Earth's atmosphere.

climate
Long-term patterns of wind, rainfall, temperature, and other aspects of day-to-day weather that change gradually over many years and centuries.

drought
A long period when little or no rain or other forms of water reach the ground.

emissions
Substances, especially gases, given off by processes such as burning fuels in cars and power stations.

environment
The surroundings, including soil, rocks, water, air, plants, animals, and even human-made structures.

greenhouse gases
Gases that help to trap heat in the atmosphere, causing the temperature of the Earth to rise.

ozone
A form of the gas oxygen, which is spread through the atmosphere and helps to protect the Earth's surface against some of the Sun's damaging ultraviolet rays.

radiation
Energy that comes from a source, like the Sun, and travels in waves, like ultraviolet (UV) rays and light rays.

smog
A combination of fumes, particles, and gases, especially from vehicle exhausts, that causes a harmful haze in the air.

275 3663